THE LEADERS TOOL BOX

APPLIED CONCEPTS OF LEADERSHIP

WRITTEN, INSTRUCTED,
AND DEVELOPED BY

TED ROGERS

ISBN: 1482039079
ISBN-13: 9781482039078

Library of Congress Control Number:
2013901200

CreateSpace Independent Publishing Platform
North Charleston, South Carolina

DEDICATION

This book is dedicated to the leaders
of the world—no matter where you are
serving and at what level!

I hold dear the men and women of this
world who wear a uniform—whether for
community or country. Whatever your
calling and specialty may be, may the
Chief be gracious to each and every one of
you and keep you safe! I have been blessed
to have been able to wear, and still do,
many different uniforms of service.

I humbly thank you for your service and leadership to mankind.

To my wife, Becky, my son, Caleb, and my extended family: you are my world; I love you more than life itself!

To the men and women with whom I have the privilege of serving—whether from the past, present, even the future. You have made and continue to make me a better person and better leader than I have ever dreamed of being!

I am forever in your debt!

CONTENTS

www.toolboxleadership.org

PREFACE

It had been a tough and very challenging year for me. I was designing and planning a leadership retreat with a wonderful group of leaders I work with. I have always believed leadership to be very dynamic, artistic, creative, and at times, completely dependent upon the given situation at hand.

Yet, the same tried and true principles of leadership are timeless; they never change, surviving all forms of challenges, even opinions of others who may disagree. Whether in the boardroom or the classroom, in times of crisis or times of calm, in your place of worship or at work, even at home, these principles resonate.

The easy part it seemed was to lecture and teach these principles to my peers; the hard part was figuring out how to visualize them as a tangible reference point so any leader could easily review these concepts to make a tough decision or just ponder on the issues before them.

We all know the immense value of alone time and finding serenity and peace to make decisions. But what if you were sitting in the office, or a hotel room, or perhaps somewhere else? I sensed the pressure to find a needed solution to portray these concepts as real!

The answer and this idea to assimilate these concepts in this manner came to me from the "Chief," which as a Christian is what I affectionately call the good Lord.

We all have a belief system of some sort and a "higher power," and I used mine to ask for help with this task. This process was my answer from the Chief, who deserves the credit!

I simply wanted to be a better leader for those that I have been given the awesome duty and privilege to lead. This box and the twenty-three concepts or tools contained herein help me do that, and I sincerely hope you find this true as well in your leadership journey. I hope it helps you as much as it does me.

For several years now, I have taught the principles and concepts of this box to the leadership groups and organizations I have been privileged to be involved with. Whether in small group settings or at conferences with many other people, the ideas have always been well received. Some folks have even told me it has changed their lives as leaders and individuals. They will never view their duties as a leader the same. I hope this is the case for you as well.

INTRODUCTION

The concepts in this book are not new, unique, or secretive. Used along with this book, they are designed to be the contents of your leadership toolbox. Some of my peers have literal boxes I made for them that they can put their hands on and dig into. I spent many hours and some funds buying these tools and things and putting this concept together. The final product was an elementary school–style pencil box with all these tools in them as a tangible lesson and concept reminder. Thus the name "toolbox."

I hope you learn from and adhere to these concepts. My desire is for you to be the best leader you can possibly be! All that you have ever learned, and ever will learn, is required to lead the men and women you come in contact with on your leadership journey.

Why a journey? Because there is no such thing as a perfect leader today on this earth, and there is no ending. Therefore, we all must strive daily to be better than we were the day before—to be a person who is worthy to teach, lead, motivate, communicate, etc.

Leadership must be lived; teaching by example is the best way. Our staff members will always do what they see us do, in spite of what we tell them to do. No pressure.

Lead on...

A Story

A child sat staring at all the "things" on the kitchen counter. He had removed them from a little box. When his father came into the room, the child asked him, "Dad, why do you have this little box of things?" His dad replied, "I am in the process of figuring that out as well."

"Dad" was one of my trusted senior staff members, and the day before, he had attended one of my "box sessions" at a leadership retreat. His son was most intrigued by the "things" in front of him. His Dad explained that each "thing" represented an important leadership concept that great leaders always use.

This book uses critical and strategic tools for your success. As you move through this book, I want to you to picture holding in your hands the very tools I am describing. I encourage this visualization because the concept and the application is of utmost importance. Frame of reference is essential and required. Each tool is a metaphor of a leadership concept.

In the beginning, I built each box by hand and gave them and the ensuing class as a gift to key members of my staff—a literal hands-on example of how to reference and apply my concepts. I am way past that now—not enough boxes, too many leaders—thus, the writing of this book.

I have written this book to be your toolbox—a desk reference, if you will, for when you need it. The more you review it, the deeper its meaning will be at any given time. The concepts herein mean different things at different times along your journey, and they will continue to plant seeds of leadership within you.

I have some peers who keep an actual box either by their nightstands, in their desk, in their back packs, or in a special, private drawer at work or at home. Peers have told me endless stories of how they have made some decisions—yes, some very tough ones—by simply examining the tools from their own box. I want you to have your own story. A story by which you use this book (or your own box) to make decisions and lead out in a better way! If you want to be an effective, successful leader, and I will show you that you can, you deserve some congratulations. You see...

YOU are an ORIGINAL!

YOU are SPECIAL!

YOU are CUSTOM-MADE!

There is no one else like you! No one possesses the skill set you do. You have gifts that you are better at than anyone else! We all are designed to excel at different things. That is the beauty of teamwork!

Whether you have a degree or not, vast experience or not, a big title or not, this should in no way diminish your ability to lead! Your ability to lead is based upon the effective use of the concepts described in this book, and the way I am presenting them to you coupled with all of your life experience, talent, and yes education, both formal and informal.

Leadership and management are not the same!

Leadership is "artistic" or creative in nature!

Management is "scientific" or methodical in nature!

Yes, the two go hand in hand, but they are vastly different.

Management science has evolved along with technology to the point where it seems we can compute ourselves out of a job! We can generate enough data sets to make it impossible for a leader to make a decision! We can literally overload a person in a leadership position with information, statistics, scenarios, and the proverbial "what if?"

"Analysis paralysis" could be the order of the day.

I am not saying this is necessarily a bad thing, because data is very valuable and needed. I have even heard the saying, "in God we trust; all others bring data!"

I am saying that data should never be the final answer; data should be used in conjunction with the tools in your toolbox, things found in this book.

Colin Powell once said that "great leaders are almost always great simplifiers."

Thus, enter the world of a small boy as we examine key concepts of leadership in a world full of things or tools used as metaphors.

Lead on...

"THE RUBBER BAND"

I believe people are like rubber bands.

They come in all shapes, sizes, colors, strengths, and styles.

Sometimes, folks get tossed around like a package of rubber bands. People are saved to be used later, like a rubber band placed around an arm. They can be snapped at people to cause damage, such as a child might use them. Or they may just feel used or taken advantage of in an organization, like part of the office supplies.

But to me, a very important thing about a rubber band or a person is simply this: in order to use one correctly and to one's best potential, one must first be stretched and grown, but never broken.

A broken rubber band or a person that is abused and broken in spirit is going to struggle rising to his full potential.

To stretch, or to grow, is paramount; if you are failing to grow as a leader, as an individual, then you are going to struggle with the challenges of leadership, and life, for that matter. Yes, there will always be things that confound us, but we must be willing to stretch our minds and grow our knowledge and experience in order to excel.

As leaders, we must do this continually for our crews, but we must be careful. We can place such pressure on our crews that they break and therefore fail. Great leaders will have a safety net such as good policy and procedures, a quality training program and back up personnel in place in case this happens so the organization and the crew member thrive.

To build an environment whereby folks can fail and learn is paramount. But the mistake or failure must not be so that "system failure" is the case. In the words of the flight director of *Apollo 13*, "Failure is not an option."

As a young boy, I assisted my mother with her hobby of ceramics. One of the tedious tasks in making ceramics is to place many rubber bands around the mold where the "slip" is then poured into. The rubber bands had to be strong, and we used several. We worked hard to stretch these rubber bands around the molds for proper application. At times, some of the rubber bands would fail, but the others would not.

So it is with people; they work best when stretched and allowed to grow. But they and the organization struggle if they are pressed to the point of failure. Have a safety net in place. Grow you crews. Stretch their minds. Your crew is the organization, and stretching is how both are made strong.

Like the country song says, "Be strong enough to bend."

Lead on...

"THE STAR"

Picture in your mind, if you will, a small, plain, cardboard star box with a removable lid surrounded by a rubber band.

This star represents a brand new crew member, one who has been assigned to your team and who plans to help you succeed. She is a "star" because she already possesses skill sets and knowledge no matter how new she is. Every organization is sitting on boatloads of talent. Just because a person is new, or is really a fresh set of eyes, does not mean she can't contribute immensely to your organization.

I have heard it said before that "talent knows no rank!"

And if you're the new guy, what do you know? Perhaps more than you realize. Every person has a unique set of life experiences, probably different from yours, and can always offer you, at the very least, an opportunity to learn and observe. I have observed on several occasions that vastly experienced folks cannot see the obvious issue in front of them or understand some other concept. A friend of mine said he could not get a mower started until, finally, someone sat in the seat, and then the thing cranked right up! Safety systems at their best! Sometimes we can be masters of the obvious...or not.

You can add to stars and make them whatever you want, grow them how they need to be grown, and even alter their design and grow their talent. But you must first realize that every single one of your teammates is a star in their own right.

Before you can remove the lid to see what is inside every employee, you must first remove the rubber band. Thus, back to the lesson of the rubber band. You must be willing to properly grow and stretch the new crew member in order to see them succeed and discover the secrets of what is inside—this includes stretching and opening your own mind as well.

Remove the lid of the star, and you will find two things inside of every one of them. The first is a tiny sponge.

Crew members, like sponges, just soak up whatever they are around. It's human nature. So the question becomes, "What are your crew members soaking up?" What is the culture of your organization like? Who will be training them and leading them, and who will they be working with or mentored by? Are they absorbing fine wine or urine?

It is absolutely imperative that you are aware and on top of your organizational culture! Culture is to the organization what blood is to the human body. If your blood is sick, you are sick—trust me. Your blood flows all through your body, affecting everything! So it is with your organizational culture; if your culture is bad, then your effectiveness will be bad or nonexistent.

Why would you take a brand new star and place them in an environment to fail? Organizations do this every day, and sometimes they don't even know it. Sometimes they do and then they wonder what went wrong?

The other item inside your star is a candle. It has been said that you cannot curse the darkness until you have lit someone's candle.

In other words, you cannot complain unless you are first willing to help and/or teach someone. As you light the flame by teaching, you must guard the flame so it does not go out. In survival training you are taught certain skills about how to start a very small fire and grow it into an effective way to stay warm, survive, or even signal your location. Guarding the flame is important, but if you guard too closely or smoother it, you will get burned or the fire will go out. Remember the terms "fire in her eyes" and "fire in his belly"? Those ideas came from someone and were passed along. You catch a cold like you catch a belief; you get it from somebody. Fire is a tool. I have seen the effective uses of fire, and I have certainly seen the destructive forces of fire. Fire is not the problem. How it is used and controlled is always the issue.

Have you lit someone's fire? Have you properly given her the tools to use and control it? Have you guarded that flame but not smothered it?

Fire stands for someone's motivation. How have you benefited someone's motivation? I certainly hope you are giving joy and not stealing it!

Your stars, many times, are what you make them. You as a leader will certainly have an effect on your stars, so the question becomes, how have you prepared them to prosper for themselves and the organization? An astute leader always knows that she is helped by people to either fail or succeed.

The stars will treat the customers the way the leadership treats them! What a concept; they will do what they see and feel regardless of what you tell them to do. Treat the staff well, and they will take care of the customer—and then success will be at your doorstep.

I was hired by an organization one time to give a mandatory customer service class to the staff, as I have done with other organizations. It seemed that the management of the organization was getting a substantial number of customer service–related complaints, and they wanted to put a stop to this.

On the first day, as I was being introduced, I read the room and noticed clearly and without a doubt that the crew did not want to be there. In fact they were required to be there. The situation was somewhat hostile. I had my work cut out for me. As I observed things and listened to people, management, and staff, the obvious came into clear view.

The crew will treat the customer the way management treats the crew.

As we will cover more in-depth later on, the crew members, and the customer all will suffer greatly if management does not understand the above concept and instead concentrates on being managers, not leaders.

Lead on...

"THE MIRROR"

I believe the mirror is the most effective leadership tool ever created and also the most underutilized.

To take a look in the mirror sounds like an old, sarcastic line. While that may be true, in reality, every leader needs to be able to take a long, hard look in the mirror. For some, this long, hard look could end up being painful but transformative as a leader.

I pray this is the case for you. Frankly, it takes a high level of intestinal fortitude, better known as guts, to take a long look and examine yourself: your flaws, things about you that are not so pretty. You may even see some failures, some things you did wrong and wish you could go back in time and change.

Your reflection is skewed from the start. We tend to see ourselves not as others see us but how we want to be seen. We all have a blind spot, things about us that others see but we do not. Remember, there are no ugly babies in the eyes of a mother.

Our self-image is, at times, what we desire to see. This is good and a place to grow into. But rest assured, there are things in that mirror that are tough to digest. As leaders, we must first accept that while we have a certain set of talents, skills, and knowledge, if we are truly worth our weight in gold, then we will understand that it is not what we know that is important but what we *do not* know. You begin to grow immensely as a leader when you realize you don't know what you don't know!

Confusing? Not really. You will fall flat on your face, and so will the team you are leading, if you do not remain humble and teachable. You may get away with this for a while, but the day of reckoning will rear its ugly head.

Just as you see your reflection, your team is a reflection of you. They are built to your standard because they are following you. What is your standard? We have already established you are a talent, you are custom-made, you are unique, you are simply you! Therefore, please realize that the leader and the crew will mirror each other. You reflect upon one another but also understand that everything, and I mean *everything*, begins and ends with leadership. Always has been, always will be.

In survival training, one of the most important tools you can have at your disposal is a mirror. It is an enormous rescue signaling device by reflecting the sun. So I ask you: What are you reflecting to your team? What higher calling or power are you reflecting? What is the essence of your character that others see in you?

As a leader, you can use the mirror to show your crew members what they need to see about themselves in order to grow and improve. But as you show others and help them with their reflections, are you just as willing to let others help you see your true reflection so you can grow and be better?

Lastly, are you willing to examine yourself first and foremost after a failure or if your team is struggling? Leaders who have the courage to do this will find their success rate explode upward for themselves and their crew.

Be that leader; be the one to set the example. Be the tide that lifts all boats. Be the one with the guts to say, "I will have the courage to examine myself first, and by doing so, I will have then earned the right to examine my crew."

Lead on...

"THE COMPASS"

Most folks know that a compass is supposed to point north. There is north, true north, and other types of north. But for the purpose of our leadership discussion, we will just concentrate on the label of "true north."

What is true north in leadership? Simply put, your compass is your heart. Is it where it should be?

Put another way, where is your heart, and do you have the right motives as you lead your crew? Great leaders always shoulder the blame and share the credit. If the crew fails, then the leader steps up and is accountable. If the crew wins, the leader says, "Look what my crew did!"

"Where is your heart?" can be just as tough a question to answer as "What do you see in the mirror?" (By now you clearly see that all of your tools work together for your betterment and complement each other.)

You can see people's behavior, but you cannot always see their motive. Your motive and the true meaning of your behavior is, of course, character based (as we'll examine later on in The Glue Stick chapter). The question of "Where is your heart?" requires so much reflection that it may take some time to answer it along your leadership journey.

As time passes, you should always be able to do a quick gut check and know with extreme certainty that your heart is pointing true north and your intentions to make something better are pure.

Does this mean you can't fire or replace somebody, tear apart a project and rebuild it better, or look for a work-around to accomplish a goal in a timelier manner?

The short answer is no. You need to be doing something for the right reason. Your heart needs to be in the right place. Your heart guides your actions. Guess what? If it's not, others will find you out. That deep, dark secret will come out, and you will be discredited. You will lose and perhaps take your loyal crew down with you.

Your crew members and peers know you better than you think. Little glimpses of our character come out about us all the time whether we realize it or not.

As a leader, you and your crew must be able to stand and deliver the products of team work and multiple skill sets in many different environments. To be *adaptive* and *audible* (like a team quarterback quickly changes a play when he sees something he does not like) is paramount for any team to function well.

Leader's share where their heart is by simply living out loud who they are and what they are. Many leaders know what leadership is, but that is only half of the issue. The other half is simply this: do you live it? Leaders who do not practice what they preach are doomed for failure.

To paraphrase St. Francis of Assisi: we should preach incessantly and, if necessary, use words.

Folks, always live it and be the example that others want to live by and serve beside.

Where is your heart?

Are you true north?

Success lies here…

Lead on…

"The Wisdom Tooth"

Wisdom; some say you become wise by experience, which is making mistakes and learning from them. I am a living testament to this, and perhaps you are as well. More importantly, wisdom and its cousin, judgment, are paramount to success.

Why the wisdom tooth?

The answer is simple. If we do not use sound judgment and apply our wisdom when making leadership decisions, this could, and many times does, come back to bite us! Thus, the wisdom tooth!

To be effective in using your wisdom and judgment, you need another cousin to these two: confidence. Confident leaders project a self-assured air. One could argue that some arrogant leaders have been successful. I would offer a counterargument.

Crews quickly know the difference between someone who is smart versus a smartass.

Confident, wise, and smart leaders are endearing to their crews. Smartasses are just that and will not get the best fruits from their crews.

Don't be arrogant; please be humble and teachable, which, trust me, is a much better example to set and for others to follow.

Yes, a leader can be tough and demanding, but here's the thing: if your crew knows your heart, trusts your judgment, and believes in you, they will put out fires as they follow you through hell and back.

Conversely, they just tolerate a smartass only for as long as they have to. This type of leader is just a blip on the radar screen, a puff of smoke that will soon evaporate. Too many times I've watched leaders fail because of this.

I am about your success, not your failure.

Many leaders draw strength from their "higher power" of choice. I certainly do and am in no way ashamed of it. I clearly understand this, and through the blessings of my higher power, experiences, education, and training, I am much better equipped to be the very best leader I can possibly be. King Solomon was reported to be the wisest man to have ever lived. Many rulers sought after his wisdom, judgment, and counsel. Perhaps we as leaders should pray for a portion of King Solomon's wisdom.

Earlier, we discussed the problem of analysis paralysis and how it can be detrimental to your leadership ability. Leaders who require more data to make a decision, and then want even more data before they move, will simply fail. Data sets change, conditions change, situations change, and there will never be enough "correct" data, or perhaps there will be too much data. The answer to this problem, which is more common than you think, is never making a leadership decision based only on data. Why?

Data, facts, figures, and statistics are scientific.

True leadership is artistic and creative.

Crew members are not numbers, although you are responsible for a number of them.

They haves senses and can smell fear, see hesitation, hear doubts, taste bittersweet failure, and touch each other with their misery. But a leader does have that "sixth sense" (trust me, it's there) and can plot a course by applying judgment and wisdom to data, facts, and statistics.

Examine the data and conditions, apply your wisdom and judgment, trust your gut, and then lead out. Do this in order without fail. My biggest screw-ups occurred when I did not trust my gut or I relied too much on data.

Lead out, boldly and confidently, having faith and believing in yourself and your crew.

Would you follow you? Interesting question, huh? If you would not follow you, why in the world would you expect your crew to follow you?

You and your crew have much to accomplish, and you will do so by applying your wisdom in all situations.

Lead on...

"Leadership Glasses"

"Without vision, the people perish," says the Bible.

All leaders know the absolute need for vision. To be able to see the landscape is imperative. Some of our greatest leaders in all walks of life have been described as visionaries. When you put on your proverbial leadership glasses, what do you see?

One of the best ways to speak about vision is to dream and think out loud. This may seem too simple, so allow me to pause for effect and say that again.

Dream and think out loud with your crew!

Leaders cast vision like fishermen cast hooks! They dream and think out loud so their crews know what they see. Not every person has to understand your vision as a leader, but they do have to believe in you!

You are their vision many times, whether you realize this or not.

Without your leadership glasses and your compass, you will be lost. People will follow you if they believe in your dream, your vision, and your heart, which are your motives.

Vision is your internal roadmap for your never-ending leadership journey. Why? Because you are always going somewhere, growing, learning, building up others, taking calculated risks, applying your wisdom and judgment, teaching—leading!

Sometimes our vision gets blurry, and we might need to do a gut check. Seek counsel from other leaders, consult your crew members about their thoughts, reexamine your motives, and ensure your heart is where it should be. Pull all the tools together from your leadership toolbox, and together they will send you down the right path.

There is nothing wrong with needing to refocus your vision. On the contrary, a great leader will welcome this refocus to ensure she is on the right path.

Vision is required.

Your leadership glasses will allow you to focus on the path forward if you are willing to listen to your wisdom, open your heart, seek counsel as needed, and be willing to see what is right in front of you.

Remember to share your vision; your crew should never wonder what you are thinking or what direction they are going. Everyone's path should be true north. Our destination, you could say, is the North Pole, the pinnacle of true north.

Even Santa Claus knows that!

Lead on...

"The Flag"

While on your leadership journey, which, by now, we have established is never ending, you will constantly be challenged. Two of the most important concepts you will have to answer for as a leader are:

Where do you stand?

What do you stand for?

I am reminded of a country song sung by Aaron Tippin that says:

You've got to stand for something or you'll fall for anything

You have to be your own man, not a puppet on a string

Never compromise what's right, and uphold your family name.

You've got to stand for something or you'll fall for anything.

I chose the flag for this concept because as a leader you will have to "post your colors" declaring what you stand for and where you stand. If you cannot or are not willing to do this, then, my friend, you are not fit to lead!

Harsh words, but better to hear them now from me than to fail during an important leadership task and disappoint yourself and those you were charged to lead.

We posted a flag on the prairie, on the moon, on the battlefield, in the classroom, in the halls of government, in our hearts, and many other places.

Posting a flag is about leadership. It says, here we are; here is what we claim or where we stand. As a leader, my position is here; come join me, or get ready to debate, fight for, or defend your position.

Leaders always know where they stand.

If you are in doubt, you do not have long to figure it out. But you must figure it out and post your flag, or you won't be the leader for long.

If you dare to dream out loud, cast vision, and say, "We are going this way" or "This is where we stand," then the mission is clear. Perhaps the details may need to come together, but you know where you are and where you are going.

President Kennedy said we would go to the moon and safely return. He planted the flag in our hearts and minds, and before the end of that decade, we as a nation planted a flag on the moon.

Where is your flag? The symbolism of the flag is all encompassing, from the flag of a nation, to the flag of your integrity, to the flag of your business, company, and certainly your crew.

To post your colors is, and should be, a very special thing. The posting of your flag speaks of your values, beliefs, and norms. It speaks of your culture and your way of business, and it defines your way forward or how you may have arrived. It is your "brand" as a leader.

It is perfectly acceptable to say to your crew, "Because I am able to and have the time, and because we are not in crisis mode,

I am thinking about this situation more in depth and will render a decision later."

Make sure "later" does come, and delay only if you truly do have time to wait.

Remember, no decision is a decision not to decide. You always and must make a decision and take a stand.

Leaders always will post their colors, take a stand, and make it clear where they are.

Lead on...

"THE WATCH"

In discussing the watch, we will think on two areas: time and timing. These are very different, very distinctive applications.

TIME

Time is too valuable; it is your most precious commodity.

Time is irreplaceable.

Time cannot be paid back, not even with interest such as with money. If I borrow your money and give it back to you with a healthy interest rate of, say, 20 percent, then you have done well in your return on investment.

But if I waste the time you "spend" on or with me, no matter what I wish for or what I may give you or how hard I try, I cannot give you back your time. It's not possible.

Take for example me arguing that living a healthful lifestyle could increase your longevity; which is very true and I totally support. But, there is no guarantee of that, and I still cannot give you back the time I took from you. Wasting your entire day on issues unrelated to work is not something a leader should be proud of.

Leaders may think that multitasking, technology, and other applications save time, and that, again, is true to a point.

The problem is that time continues to continually tick away. Like a thief in the night, it takes and takes and takes while we live our lives and make our plans.

I have heard before that if you want to make God laugh, tell him your plans.

Time can be measured, divided up, shared, treasured, stolen, examined, and enhanced. It can even be forgiven by not charging you more of it, such as a commuted prison sentence.

But once time is used, spent, or given, time is lost—forever.

True leaders do not waste people's time. No matter how good you are, you can never, under any circumstance, pay or give it back.

Leaders keenly examine systems regarding the use of time closely. They understand the virtual dynamic of not just time management but the inherit value of time. How time is used, divided up, and spent.

Time is a form of currency—valuable currency—and we all spend it in many different ways.

How do you spend your time? More importantly, as a leader, how do you spend the time of your crew?

Therefore, I believe that one of the many precious gifts a person can give you is his or her time. Since you cannot repay it, how do you receive or spend it? What do you do with such a precious gift?

There are so many stories of folks on their deathbed saying they wish they had not done this or that. Their regrets about time include working too much, not planning adequately for financial security, not spending enough time with the kids, or taking up too much time worrying, perhaps about nothing, as it turned out.

I have heard divorcing spouses saying, "I gave you the best years of my life," and students saying, "I spent too much time goofing off and should have studied more." There are as many time stories, good or bad, as there are stars in the sky. What is your time story? Only you really know.

Effective and genuinely great leaders know their time story. They also know the time story of their crew. Many people "spend" their working lives giving a substantial amount of time to their peers and employers.

Bosses want us to use time wisely; we want to do the same. I have a great relationship with the crews I work with, but I am not naïve enough to think that they would want to spend their time doing other things.

Mostly, we trade our time and talents for treasure.

We work using our skill sets to obtain money so we can do the things we choose to do. What a concept! Let's make it as efficient as possible.

Why? Because time sneaks up on you—tick-tock, tick-tock—and the seconds pass.

TIMING

Timing is everything.

Are you familiar with the saying, "Good idea, not the right time"?

Have you ever heard someone say, "She was ahead of her time"?

How about, "Wow, who would have thought we would live to see that?"

Timing is a crucial component of time. Battlefield operations can be dependent on timing. Theatrical performances and movies can whisk us away with well-timed special effects. Speeches and debates can swing drastically according to strategically timed barbs, jokes, and important points. Promotions, resignations, business presentations, and new products can all use timing to enhance the success of the venture.

Great leaders have a keen and acute sense of timing and know how to use it to their advantage.

Countless times in my leadership journey I have used the advantage of proper timing to make presentations, submit ideas, remake plans, develop and execute a strategy or operational guideline, and design the tactics of how my crew will accomplish the task at hand. The hard part is, many times, there is no real textbook to teach one how to do this.

We do not want to go back to "analysis paralysis" or debate management-related scientific theory until the cows come home, but suffice it to say that leaders know timing is an essential secret weapon of sorts.

Proper timing can literally make or break an entire plan, operation, presentation, or product launch. "Go" or "no go" can be supported by mounds of data for and against, but in the end, every astute leader knows in his or her gut that timing is everything.

So in everything, use "time" wisely, and know the intrinsic value of "timing."

Leaders know this and always do this to the best of their ability.

Lead on...

"THE ROCK"

As a leader, you are the rock upon which the team is built.

I will let that sink in...

For quite a while...

And then some more time...

I cannot emphasize this enough. I once worked for someone who taught me that there are many different types of rock. He stated clearly that a rock is not a rock. News to me, but he was passionate about this, so I respected his views and listened.

There are many types of rocks, just like there are many types of leaders and leadership styles. The context of this book explores important concepts of leadership represented by many different tools. However, the content of this book is also about how leaders must exhibit these behaviors to be successful.

In the Bible, Peter was called a rock. Other leaders, visionaries, and trendsetters are referred to as rocks. Television commercials refer to trucks as rocks. Comparisons to rocks are too many to name in this book, but you get the picture.

So why is this? Why the rock?

Leaders, like rocks, are foundational—period.

Again: as a leader you are the rock upon which the team is built. You are foundational. You must show strength and fortitude (better known as guts), and you must lead out in a manner that shows strength of courage and character.

Builders use rocks because they last and last. Many foundations are drilled until we reach bedrock. Rocks can withstand storms and bad weather conditions and hold up well over time.

Leaders, as rocks, know folks build upon them. Scripture tells us the wise man built his house upon the rocks. Your crew will build upon you continually. Your proper use of the tools and concepts discussed within this book will always be reviewed by your crew as they build their workplace and team upon their rock: you, their leader.

Rocks can also be used as weapons. They can be deadly when harnessed in a slingshot and released to strike with leverage, momentum, and skill. They were launched from catapults during ancient times to cause destruction as they struck the walls of a city or fort. Today, people throw rocks at each other during fights and civil unrest.

When leaders are not in harmony for the greater good, they as rocks can be destructive to one another and other teams. It is said that wars start with words and that attorneys are hired when folks can no longer communicate and work out their problems. I am sorry but I don't agree with the childhood saying that "sticks and stones can break my bones, but words can never hurt me." Words can be like rocks and certainly can be used as weapons. Woe be unto the leader who cannot capture and master this concept.

As rocks, leaders can be joined together for the common good or can be destructive toward one another. Like my philosophy of the rubber band, rocks and leaders and people come in all shapes and sizes, colors, strengths, and weaknesses and can be used in so many applications.

Convicts have endured many a hard day on the rock pile breaking rocks down. Rocks are tough for the most part, and so the leader must be as well.

Are you, as they say down south, a person tough enough for someone to hang their hat on? Are you foundational? Are you the proverbial Rock of Gibraltar? Can you also be a part of a team like a rock wall?

Leaders are rocks that have strength, fortitude, and character and are made to last. And while they can be used as a weapon, leaders know that at the end of the day, they must be the foundation the successful crew builds upon.

Are you that rock? Are you there for your crew? Have they built their workplace or team upon you? Have they seen your strength and stability?

As a leader, do you know the answer to this? Because, guess what? Your crew already does!

Commit today to being the rock they need!

Lead on...

www.toolboxleadership.org

"The Glue Stick"

Have you ever heard about a crew having a "glue" that holds them together? They seem united toward a common mission, have a common bond, and exhibit the common thread of tireless teamwork. One would think they are strong and unbreakable. They seem to function with an unseen sense of purpose that portrays itself as incredibly strong.

In a way, there appears to be some type of superglue that continually mixes among them. Not the weaker glue of a Post-it

Note, but a glue that is unshakable, is strong enough to roll with the punches, reacts appropriately to different conditions, and laughs in the face of adversity. What is this mix or glue that binds the crew? It's certainly not superglue, because even it is not strong enough to fit these characteristics under these circumstances. What, pray tell, is this secret sauce?

Skilled leaders know the answer because this glue is required for success. Like Spider-Man, leaders are swinging all over the place, applying the adhesive, and latching on to people and things. Superglue from a super hero: is it a secret sauce? No.

Character is the answer. The leader's character is the glue that is so strong and so noticed among the successful crew. More importantly, it is the leader's character that is most visible.

www.toolboxleadership.org

Volumes upon volumes have been written about the importance of a leader having good character.

I teach all the crews I have the privilege to lead about what I call the three Ps. Woe unto you if you are guilty of abusing one or more of the three Ps. Many a good man and woman have failed as a leader, or a person, for that matter, because they misused the three Ps. They are:

Pleasure   **Power**   **Purse**

Leaders abuse their desire for *pleasure* either through inappropriate relationships, substance abuse, or being vicious toward others in so many different ways and taking joy from it.

Leaders abuse their *power* (covered next as The Bomb tool) and do the wrong things toward their crew or employer, or perhaps they abuse their power by not realizing that a true leader never really wants power. Abraham Lincoln, our sixteenth president of the United States, said, "If you want to test a man's character, give him absolute power."

Leaders who abuse the *purse* by desiring too much money, exhibiting greed, taking too much, swindling their investors, misusing company funds, buying to excess, or abusing money in some over the top manner will fail miserably by such behavior.

Sadly, I have seen many people in my life fail in so many different situations by abusing one or more of the three Ps. Don't let it be you...please.

Headlines and leading stories in the media talk all the time about how a leader failed and succumbed to the three Ps. Yes, we are all human and subject to make mistakes, but simply be aware that when failure occurs, too many times it is related to these three things.

Character is the secret sauce that holds the crew and organizations together and launches enormous success. More importantly, when we speak of character in this context, we are talking about the character of the leader.

I believe we are all leaders; the only question is: at what level in the organization do you serve? That's right: serve. It has been said that champion tennis players are the ones who have the best serve.

What's your serve like as a leader? Another important question is what or whom do you serve?

Remember the previous tools and how they all work together? Where is your compass or heart? What is your organization's culture, and what are the stars soaking up in the sponges inside them?

The character of the leader permeates the entire organization. The crew will be who you are and do what you do in spite of what you tell them. You will make mistakes, yes. But if they know you are true north, that your motive is pure, that you are a rock they build upon, and that you are not afraid to look in the mirror before you ever look at them, a strange and glorious thing happens.

Your crew will know you and forgive your mistakes. Some things, unfortunately, are not repairable, but not most things. Thankfully, most mistakes are repairable, and the crew and leader can heal and move on.

The secret sauce enabling the leader's successes is strong, steadfast, foundational, ethical character.

The cousin to character is integrity. They go hand in hand with the leader. I use a simple measure to define and analyze integrity: what will you do when you know without a doubt you won't get caught? Your choice of actions during times like these is precisely indicative of your level of integrity.

As a great leader, it is a must that you be a stellar rock of character and integrity.

Sadly, you and your crew can fall flat on your faces due to the lack of solid character and quality integrity.

What strength does your glue stick have?

Having good character and integrity is much like being pregnant—there's no middle ground there. You're either pregnant or not. You either have character and integrity or not.

Lastly, please avoid trying to fool yourself and the rest of us by faking good character and integrity. The truth will always find you out, and I pray that not too many people or organizations get hurt by your foolish game.

Good people and organizations deserve better.

Lead on...

"The Bomb"

Every leader has a bomb whether he realizes it or not. Leaders can do incredible damage to themselves and their organizations and, sadly, to others, innocent or not.

The bomb I am speaking of is power.

In your leadership toolbox, there is a small celebration device, such as a champagne party popper with a string for activation. This item represents a bomb of power in concept.

Make no mistake, you possess an explosive device as a leader and you can use your power to impact people's lives in unimaginable ways. If they choose to, leaders can be a wrecking ball over the workforce and the organizations where they serve.

I believe there are two best uses of your power as a leader.

The first is to make wrongs right if at all possible.

The second is to be good to people as you guide and protect your crew, leading them where you need them to be in order to improve your organization.

There again are volumes written about the many different types of power. But here is the deal: we all *get it* when someone or something has power over us. This is the context in which I want to spend our time.

My two finest examples in teaching about power and using power are the hand grenade and the boomerang. They are based upon my best uses of power described above and are examples of how I prefer to use my power as a leader.

THE GRENADE

Grenades have lots of power, and the examples of leaders using power in the form of a grenade are endless. Your power as a leader is a part of you, and you do not have to be present to use it.

Really?

Yes, really. If your crew knows what you stand for and where you stand, then your power permeates the organization's culture much like your character does.

Have you ever heard, "You'd better not do that or we'll get in trouble"? What about, "Man, that will never fly around here"? Better yet, "When she gets back, there is going to be hell to pay."

We are speaking of power here, folks, and its uses are many and varied. I am a professional clique buster. I hate cliques because they are detrimental to the organization's culture. Many times I will toss a grenade their way by showing up and explaining how folks should mingle, be kind, and stop judging so harshly, and how our differences make us stronger.

While diversity training is important, should we not also train for unity? Diversity falls right in line, and the people and the organization prosper when we really concentrate on unity and common goals. In the form of a leadership grenade, your power is very portable.

And while power is very portable, there are many different types of grenades, just like there are many types of power. Each situation has its own application and circumstances.

Sadly, there are times when a leader must shield others from the misuse of power. There are countless stories where our soldiers saved others by throwing themselves on grenades, losing life and/or limb protecting others. To even think of these sacrifices of our men and women in uniform makes me swell with pride and humble gratitude of their service and sacrifice. Heroes to the very core!

But even on an organizational level, there may be times where you will get injured protecting the crew because you showed character and planted your flag where it needed to be and it was not at all popular to take such a stand. Do it anyway! You and the group will be better for it.

As a leader, if you are worth your weight in gold, you quickly realize you are not running a popularity contest. You are tasked with leading out, so fire at will.

Lastly, power tends to corrupt. So as a leader, while you do have power, you really don't want it.

Like a grenade after the pin is pulled, once you are actually given power, you need to get rid of it, or it will blow you up and destroy you.

Use your power wisely. Remember how King Arthur was referenced once in a movie: "He wears his power so lightly; how could I not love him?" Stay humble and teachable as a leader, and know without a doubt that power in and of its very self can destroy you quickly if not held in check and used properly.

Power is a tangled mess. You need it to do your job effectively, but you really should not want it. You have to give it away for it to work properly, but then strange things happen, as we'll see in the concept below.

THE BOOMERANG

If thrown correctly, a boomerang will return to where it was propelled. Interesting; with all the talk about empowering our folks and letting them grow, I find this to be an amazing example. Yes indeed, you have to give away your power and empower your crew. Because power corrupts so often, many shared power concepts have been created in organizations, nations such as ours, and in businesses and groups all over the world. We have three branches of government, and no one gets elected king, so the three branches share that power according to the US Constitution.

As a leader, you are wise to use a shared power concept and empower your crew and other leaders in the organization. I throw the boomerang of power everyday in the multiple groups and teams I work with.

But it always comes back, many times more powerful! What to do?

The trick is to keep throwing it away, thus the boomerang concept. Power comes back because it is properly thrown and used. It comes back because of your humble heart and stellar ethics and solid character. It comes back because your crew does a good job and says, "Hey, what can we do next?"

You have to keep giving power away all the time. You do want it to come back so you can inspect it and see if it was used properly. If necessary, adjust anything or repair the concept of empowering.

One of the biggest ways leaders screw up the use of power is sending a crew to do a task and holding them accountable but without giving them the necessary authority or power to get the job done. It's like in sales: lots of folks in an organization can say no, but you are trying to get to the person who can say yes!

The same is true of leaders who desire power and love being in charge but who don't want to be held accountable. Great leaders are always willing to be held accountable.

You have heard before that managers do things right and leaders do the right thing; very true. But it is even more true that managers *count* and leaders are *accountable*.

Wear you power lightly, realize the awesome power you have over people's lives, and practice the best uses every day. Make wrongs right, be good to people, and lead them properly.

Lead on...

"Gold"

How do you spend your gold as a leader?

What is your gold in the leadership context of this book and your leadership toolbox?

Your gold is your talent—the many skill sets you possess. Remember, you trade your time using your gold for other treasure, as in money. What can you do with your gold? As a leader, you are required to use it by giving it away, realizing you will never run out.

Why is your gold so powerful? Because your many talents are so powerful.

In your box, you have seven pieces of gold. Why seven pieces?

Because there are seven days in a week; you must use your leadership gold and talents every day without fail! Great leaders are always on the job, even at home or in contact with complete strangers at the store. Indeed, it is exhausting to be a great leader!

To whom do you give your gold? Everyone you touch, teach, train, groom, grow, build, foster, and make better than when you found them. As a leader, you impact people's lives—every day whether you realize it or not. No pressure, but it's true.

You have to stand and deliver the product of teamwork and improve people's skill sets. Just by being around them, you can and should make them better on the inside and out.

Gold and time are commodities; they are precious and in limited supply by their very nature. Folks, your talents are very precious, and you are custom-made. There is something you can do better than anyone else. Please know, like gold, you are truly precious, even if you don't like to think that way.

The talent inside of you must spring forth in such a manner that folks know that your intentions are pure and that you are here for the greater good. We are all special. I have heard it said that only with the heart can one see rightly. What is truly important is invisible to the naked eye. There's another tool: your compass. Where is your heart? Are you true north?

You will always find what you are looking for. If you desire a fight, get ready, because somebody will give you that. If you desire peace, it's out there, although, sadly, it might take a fight to get it sometimes.

Many times we forget to simply give away the very thing we desire. Love, money, security, peace, happiness—all are there waiting for you, especially if you give that very thing away first so that someone else can have it.

You will never be truly happy or successful in your life until you can be genuinely happy for others in the same way you desire.

To whom do you give your gold? The answer reminds me of a one-word speech I heard was given once at a Salvation Army convention: "others."

You give your leadership gold to others. Every day.

Lead on...

"The Battery"

We all have an internal battery. We all have an energy force within us that powers us forward and fuels dreams, motivations, and desires. However, the energy force I am speaking about regarding your internal leadership battery is your soul force.

We are all leaders in some capacity, as I have mentioned earlier. What becomes of your soul force energy level as you go about your daily business with all those around you? Just being around people many times is, simply, draining. Being a great leader is exhausting work. Your focus, your attention, your skill set, and your talent are compromised when you are too tired.

The power level of this soul force—the leadership battery—is high, medium, or low, depending upon the person and the situation.

Passion, or soul force, is what really drives us all. Of all the things that keep us going and charge up our energy reserves, what we are passionate about is the fuel of our fire, if you will.

What are you passionate about?

One of my trusted fellow leaders and I once discussed a concern we had about folks being committed to our crew and mission. We wondered if we should question people's level of commitment or not.

www.toolboxleadership.org

In the end, we decided that all were committed on the crew but that each one of them had an obviously different level of passion for the team and its mission as compared to the rest of their lives. This is completely normal and one of the things leaders face every day.

This is very important. Your passion drives you. Your values are served and come to fruition when you inject a healthy dose of passion.

As a leader, you have immense power and the ability to generate enormous emotions and create an environment where your crew can motivate themselves and accomplish the many tasks at hand.

One of the critical mistakes a leader can make is getting caught up in the process of competing. Stop this. Get busy creating.

Remember, leadership is artistic, not scientific. Great leaders and artists create things.

How do you as a leader stay charged up enough to give away your passion and have enough reserves for yourself and still motivate others and bring out their passion and motivation? This is the age-old question, is it not? If we could answer this and confidently predict which way the squirrel was going to go on the roadway, we could all retire to the beach!

Folks, I believe the answer is this: while understanding you can't give away what you do not have, you still must constantly dream out loud, share your desires, cast vision, plot a course, and tell the crew.

I have heard it said before that if you want to go to sea, do not tell the crew to build a boat; instead, teach them to long for the sea.

Create an environment and foster an organizational culture where they want to go to sea with you, and, together, you will get there. For any project, any task, you must cast vision and state the desired outcome and the motivations for it, and you and your crew are on your way.

This is cleansing and empowering because your heart will be on display, and your crew will catch that passion and dream, and it will feed them. Their performance will, in turn, come back and feed you, similar to the boomerang concept of power.

You are recharged to the level that you charge up others.

You feed on each other's level of passion, motivation, and commitment. When you and the crew each know you both have skin in the game, then a plan comes together. You are invested in each other.

Once, when I worked at a hospital and was going through some leadership challenges, I started feeling down and a bit depressed. Sitting at my desk, I just smiled, picked myself up, and "made rounds."

Going through the halls of a hospital can be uplifting and enforce a level of compassion, gratitude, and humbleness that is hard to describe in words. The emotions are powerful. When you think you have it bad, I challenge you as a fellow leader to go see folks in a hospital and lift folks up.

Smile, pray, bring flowers, dare to brighten someone's day. I guarantee you this: your leadership journey explodes upward to the positive with a level of immeasurable passion. You will sense the immediate level of passion's cousin: Compassion.

We have discussed earlier that you get a positive attitude like you get a cold: you catch it from somebody. Give away your passion, your soul force; give it away in such a manner that you lift and inspire others, have compassion for others. Everybody is fighting a battle in some form.

Spend you energy reserves doing good, looking in the eyes of your crew and all those around you, and sharing your dreams, casting vision, and exposing your heart and motivations.

Tell your crew what I tell my crews: I am a better person when I am around them, and I mean it.

Can you say that?

When you give away the very thing you need, in this case, part of your battery reserves of passion, you turn into a nuclear reactor on an aircraft carrier, which can steam for years and years before refueling.

You become the Energizer Bunny, spinning around, beating your drum, winking and smiling as you go about your business—leading out.

You recharge as a leader by simply recharging others.

The process is cyclical. Like you and your crew reflect each other in the mirror, you recharge each other in accomplishing your mission. Your crew feeds off of you; they will be who and what you are.

If they are passionate, it's because you are. If they are down and out, go to your toolbox, look in your mirror, and check your compass. What do they say?

After doing this, you have earned the right to adjust your crew and call yourself a leader.

Lead on…

"Crayons"

I love crayons. Do you? I love the many colors.

You know the star in your leadership toolbox we discussed before? The plain box shaped as a star that represents your team member? Yes, the one with the candle and the sponge inside, that one.

What shade would you color them? I am not speaking of race. I am speaking of the endless possibilities of the hundreds of colors and combinations and what they might represent.

I am speaking of the power to choose. Your leadership crayons represent freedom and your power of choice.

As a leader you must color, or shape and design, your crew the way you need them to be. The freedom to choose is one of your most sacred possessions. Many men and women have shed blood so that we may be free. Yes, freedom is not free; a heavy price has been paid and always will be if we are to remain free.

Leaders know this. The prized possession known as the freedom to choose is one of the greatest gifts you can be given or give to your crew. It is empowering.

This is not to say you must have a committee vote before you can do anything.

Sometimes it is appropriate to vote and check consensus.

But make no mistake, when leaders are placed in or given command, they must command.

I have had the privilege of commanding men and women over thirty years—and in some pretty hairy situations at times. I am speaking of creating an environment where your crew can color themselves and you can color, mold, and design your crew members to be the best they can be according to their talents and skill sets.

You have already taught them to know without a doubt they are special and cus-tom-made. Some folks work better as aggressive reds, mellow greens, stable earth tones, confident purple and blues, and con-trasting black, grays, and whites—perhaps even a gold color suits them best.

Work very hard to maintain your options while committing to a course of action. Make use of your freedom to choose and design the way forward. Changing out teammates based upon their strengths and weaknesses and then putting together a team by respecting the many colors and differences of people's skill sets is another artistic task of a leader.

You will find that though a person fails in one capacity, they can excel in another capacity and maintain their value to the team. One of your teammates may struggle with a task, but when moved to a different position, she wins the day. Leaders know their people and know where to "color" and "play" them. This is another reason why your crew must remain audible in every possible way.

Lead on…

"The Paintbrush"

Why is there a paintbrush in your leadership toolbox, and what does it represent
as a leadership concept? By now, you have
learned to ask this question, as all the tools
or things in this box represent an important concept of leadership.

The paintbrush is a reminder and representative of your ability as a leader to
organize, create, and construct your crew.
In other words, it's how you touch people
in a sense that you affect their lives by your
actions.

Make no mistake, as a leader you impact people's lives for the better or for the worse.

You touch people like an artist touches the canvas.

One minute there is a blank canvas, and the next, through the power of choice and creativity and the processes of design and vision, behold: a work of art comes forth and thus a passionate, motivated, and well-trained crew member stands before you.

Your touch comes about because you choose how you help construct and design your crew—each and every one of them.

As a leader, you have incredible power over people's lives and touch them in ways you cannot imagine and, perhaps, even take for granted.

Leaders can enable or destroy people's lives and passions by their actions or words.

Leaders must be careful what they say and do!

How you touch, or in the context of this book, affect others, is paramount to success—theirs and yours as a leader.

I believe and teach my crews that people quit people, they don't quit jobs; and we don't have jobs, we have relationships.

Data suggests that money is lower on the scale of desire than many may imagine. The need for recognition, appreciation, input, and feeling like a valued member of the crew is more important to job satisfaction. Yes, money is important, and we have to put food on the table, pay the rent, and put gas in the car. But also understand that people quit *you*, really, when they leave their job and move on to a place where they feel appreciated and valued. The relationship fell apart.

On the other hand, people stay with people when conditions may not be the best. They buy you, the leader, like a person buys the salesman or sales pitch, and then they buy the product or the mission and stay on to see it through.

So how do you touch people as a leader? Do you improve their lives and make them feel a part of a valued crew? Or do you steal their joy and make them wish they were somewhere else? People have accused me of being too mushy at times with this concept. I answer back, "Really? You're kidding me, right?"

One time I had an operations manager rebuff this. I told him, as an example, that women require appreciation, and men desire it. He came to work one morning and got onto the crew first thing for not having their equipment cleaned and ready for inspection before he said good morning to anyone.

www.toolboxleadership.org

He was not nice about this. The men just got up and went about their business. The women got up, looked at each other, and did the same after they said, "Well, good morning to you too!"

He learned a lesson that day: be nice even while being firm and corrective, where you are able—and mostly you are able.

Doing so pays huge dividends and reaffirms relationships in a positive manner. Remember, we don't have jobs, we have relationships—appropriate ones, of course.

As a leader, how do you touch or affect people's lives? You cannot perhaps comprehend the way you truly touch and affect your crew. How do you go about using your paintbrush on your crew? How do you create, organize, construct, design, and affect your crew for the greater good and to accomplish the mission at hand?

Leaders touch people, and you affect your crew enormously. Be cognizant of this concept, and continually reexamine how you can improve your skill set as you go about affecting the lives and relationships of your crew daily.

Lead on…

"THE TROPHY"

You've won the trophy and the award? Congratulations on your accomplishment.

To whom do you give the credit? Who do you share the trophy with? The trophy or your medal is colored gold, like your leadership gold, and is directly connected.

We have seen that you must give away your leadership gold or your talents every day by coming in contact with people, even if you are off work or not on an assignment. No days off for great leaders. We have a duty to affect people daily in a positive manner—even if it's just a big smile and a big tip!

I read a story about the legendary football coach Bear Bryant of the University of Alabama. He asked the football team, "Have you called your parents and thanked them? No one ever gets anywhere or succeeds by themselves. Call your parents and thank them."

What about you? Leaders share the credit and shoulder the blame. You have won the award, but really, did *you*?

I was humbled to the core when I received a national leadership award the first time it was ever given. I was privileged to have many of my crew present with me. I immediately thanked them and said, "No leader could ever receive such an award without realizing he was riding upon the shoulders of his crew."

To this day the award is in a space we all share, and alongside it hangs the letter I wrote dedicating that award to the many members of our leadership team and the many valued members of our crew. The award is not mine; it is ours.

To whom do you give credit to? To whom do you give your trophy? To whom do you give your gold?

I love to say, "It's about the peeps, not me or us as a senior leadership team." Do you have systems in place in your organization where you as senior leadership are not even eligible for awards? I do, and they're in all the organizations I have the privilege to lead. There are certain awards where senior staff (including myself) are not even a consideration, and the peeps, as I say, know this up front.

One such process is the equipment pot. A sum of money is set aside for the maintenance of equipment. At the end of the year, whatever money is left in the pot minus repairs or replacement of any damaged equipment is then distributed in cash to all the crew, except the senior leadership.

Newsflash: it's not about you; it's about the peeps. You may lead and drive the mission, but they accomplish the mission. As the philosopher once said, "When the leader's work is done, the people will rejoice and say, look what we did!"

Over your career as a leader, you will surely be given awards. Congratulations! The real test of leadership is deciding who you include and thank. You never accomplish anything by yourself.

Lead on...

"The Ruler"

We all tend to examine and measure things. We size up things, people, situations, and products. Measuring is in our very nature as human beings, it seems. We even cook and measure the ingredients and fine-tune them in hopes of a more perfect meal.

We gauge and measure and presume things about people, places, and things all the time. Sadly, we tend to judge too harshly and, more importantly, incorrectly.

Dr. Thomas J. Stanley researches the truly wealthy in our country, and his many books regarding the wealthy are fascinating reading. His research shows that more often than not, those who look wealthy, in our opinion, are not. You could not pick the truly wealthy, and I mean millionaires living right next door to you, out of a proverbial lineup of the rich based upon the lifestyles they lead. Stanley has completed a substantial amount of research, and it mostly seems to pivot around a central concept: as a populace, when we measure what we think are the displays of wealth, the truth is usually quite the opposite.

In my humble existence on this earth, I have learned things are not as they seem.

In fact, just as your mother may have told you, it is always dangerous to judge a book by its cover (no pun intended).

www.toolboxleadership.org

Yet as a leader, you are charged with conducting assessments and measurements. There will be reports to read or generate, data sets, benchmarking, technical analysis, formulas, and other management tools of the trade to review and apply. I know during my master's degree program, I was less than thrilled about suffering through the quantitative analysis course. I was very thrilled to graduate though!

But in all my years of experience, both formal and informal education, you can bet your bottom dollar I have learned this critical and crucial thing:

Be very careful what and how you measure something or someone.

Thus, enter the ruler as pat of your leadership toolbox. I can say with confidence that this is an area of leadership where many mistakes are made. How can I say this with such great confidence?

Because I have screwed up and seen many of my peers screw up in regard to how and what they measure, that's why!

One of the biggest issues of concern for a leader is this: what you choose to measure is what the organization and your crew will pay the closest attention to. Because they know what you are concentrating on, the crew will tend to do the same. This is tough in a way because there is so much to observe in any group or company.

In the end, it boils down to priorities and proper goal setting. I believe you know how to set goals as you apply the concepts of the tools in your leadership toolbox and from you experience. The key here is to be careful what you measure with your leadership ruler. You have to make it count and get it right because others are following suit. As carpenters say: measure twice; cut once!

Response times for firefighters are vital, but it's also important to arrive safely. Hospital cleanliness is paramount, and quality and accurate charting is required, but so is correct dosing and best practices in patient medication administration. Saving money and helping the bottom line in the company is important, but how long do you seriously forgo proper maintenance of the facility and physical plant? Can a soldier really fight a battle with .6 percent of a tank and 1.4 magazines full of ammo per weapon? The benchmarking report says we have 2.3 too many people and we have no part-timers; we have to get to ten, so let's cut three folks and come in under. Do we have to staff critical care heavy when most of the patient load is not critical, or do we need seven different types of hose and nozzles when four will be more than plenty? Is it safe to cut out personal contact time with the customer because they order a lot, or did you take that for granted? We only have a crash every three years at the airport, so we are good, right? The list of examples can go into perpetuity.

As a leader, decide what you want to measure, then make it count, and, by all means, do the right thing! Others are depending upon you to get it right.

Lead on...

www.toolboxleadership.org

"THE TROWEL"

Some of you may be asking, "What's a trowel?" A trowel is a hand tool used by a mason to work with concrete, bricks, mortar, block, stone, etc.

I want you to picture in your mind a brick wall. The major components of this wall are the bricks, mortar mix (concrete mixture), and the craftsman who will build the wall.

The bricks are your crew members; the mortar mix is the culture and the many processes of your crew and organization. The leader is the craftsman.

Yes, the bricks must be of good quality. The mortar mix has to be just right in order to work effectively. The craftsman must be highly skilled and know how to build and construct the wall (or team).

In its most simple form, this is any organization. If the wall or organization fails, the bricks or people mostly survive, the bad mortar mix can be cleaned away, and the bricks are retrained and used again.

The mortar cannot be used again as before. What did the leader or craftsman do wrong in building the wall for it to fail?

When a group fails, it is because the leadership failed.

Perhaps the leader did not have the skill set required as a craftsman to build the organization properly.

Perhaps the leader was properly skilled but failed to properly mix the mortar of the organization.

The mortar mix of an organization is quite extensive. There are so many things, from policy and procedure, to training and skill sets. The poor culture of an organization can cause it to fail with the best controls in place if the leader does not lead effectively.

If you are a leader and have never watched a craftsman build a wall, you need to. The master craftsman is always examining, adjusting, measuring, and adding and taking away mortar mix while using his trowel in a blur of activity. He is constantly on the move, selecting bricks, accepting some, rejecting some, placing the bricks carefully, adding just the right amount of mortar, and ensuring proper alignment and position. If it's not right, he tears it out and fixes it before the mortar sets and becomes too difficult to fix later. A substantial effort is made to get it right the first time, and then system checks happen as he moves on. He returns to measure and ensure that section of the job or even a single brick is right compared to the mortar and other bricks around it. He understands that every brick, as well as the mortar mix, affects all the other bricks.

The leader should emulate the masonry craftsman, doing the same with her crew and organization.

Leaders build people. People build the team while the leader is busy building and investing in people.

I have never spent a day building a team and I work with several teams. I spend every day I can building the people on the team because they are the team. As the leader, my job is to build and groom the people. The team comes together as the crew members invest in and accept each other.

As a leader, what are you building?

Do you have the courage to use your trowel with excessive detail and skill? If not, are you willing to increase your skills so you can be a master craftsman?

Your trowel, similar to the paintbrush, is your ability to touch and alter the people and processes of your organization.

Leadership is about building and creating and having the vision of the wall in your mind.

At times, your trowel will represent your experience and the many trials and tribulations you will go though as a leader and master craftsman. You have to get some mud on you through your trials to be effective and have great skill. Just like every US Marine is a rifleman, every leader is a craftsman. Be a master. Dream—and build.

Lead on…

"Seeds"

Leaders are farmers in many ways. They are continually planting seeds. Crops must have good seed in the ground with fertile soil, and other conditions, such as moisture, are paramount.

Seems everybody wants a harvest, but so few put seed in the ground. It takes work to farm and work to put seed in the ground and work to invest in others.

Seed in the leadership context is representative of your investment in others.

Have you put seed in the ground so your crew and organization can grow and you all, therefore, can reap the harvest of success or profits? Successful outcomes just don't happen by themselves or automatically.

Research and development in an organization is farming, finding a better way, making the investment, and reaping the harvest. Seed is put in the ground.

The four most powerful things on this earth seem to be fire, wind, water, and compound interest. When each of these grows and is out of control, oh my, get ready; here comes an interesting day.

I told my son about the power of compound interest when I was teaching him to invest his money in appreciating assets. Albert Einstein called compound interest a man made wonder of the world.

We have discussed that leaders build people and the people build the team. I consider this to be one of the true secrets of leadership. So many leaders mistakenly focus on the team or the field when actually the seeds of success that need to be planted for the harvest are within the investment, building, and planting of the crew members themselves.

Leaders of the world, you must put some seed in the ground in order to reap a harvest. I know this is obvious and sounds so simple, but so few do it. Who are you building and investing in?

Many leaders want wealth but don't put forth extra effort or make sacrifices to invest in their people. They fail to see that this "seed money" will one day work harder than they do as it grows and compounds. It works just like personal finances. Just a few thousand dollars planted early in your twenties in quality investments, left alone to grow at a decent rate of return for many years, has a great chance of being a large amount of money, a great harvest. When folks see this example, they get mad and say, "Man, I wish I had done that," or "Why didn't they teach me this in school?"

So why do we have trouble planting seeds and investing in people? We all want a harvest, so why the delay?

Plating seeds is hard work and, like investing, involves risk, as every seed planted will not produce a yield. But take the risk and invest your dollars and invest in your crew. The harvest will be plentiful if you faithfully invest and expect a return in your crew.

Build people...again...and again...and again.

Have the courage to put some seed in the ground like the farmer. The harvest will come, and the tree will bring forth fruit. Have that faith. It is worth the effort given—many times over.

Lead on...

"The Spring"

I believe leaders are springs and, more importantly, must act as springs. To understand this concept, we must begin once again with a question relative to observation.

Have you watched a spring function in a machine? Machinists are very skilled and intelligent folks. Machines and robots operate with incredible precision. Usually, a spring is attached in at least two ways to moving parts. They are hooked in and attached to allow certain levels of ranges and movements for the machine to operate properly.

Therefore, the spring allows the machine to function in a predetermined range of motion and actions. Springs come in all shapes and sizes and in various forms and strengths.

Springs are hooked to machine parts like leaders are hooked to people. They stretch and contract, ensure precision, and allow the latitude whereby the machine or crew is allowed to function.

Leaders are not only springs themselves, but they can insert springs into organizations by the prudent use of policy, procedure, operational guidelines, and system checks. Even in investing, you can place an order that triggers a sell on your stock if it falls below a certain amount of value to protect your investment dollars.

Leaders as springs must calibrate their organizations to a certain level while allowing a range of freedom and motion so the crew can grow and learn and reach new levels of understanding and success.

Leaders must be precise at times in dealing with the crew, such as disciplinary issues. An example of this is one of my favorite leadership topics, which I call "shotgun management." Allow me to use a simple illustration only relating to how different weapons function in this context of leadership.

Say, for instance, a crew member does something wrong, and he deserves corrective measures and discipline. I have seen so many leaders "fix" the problem by creating a policy because someone screwed up, so now the whole crew has to deal with this policy. Now, at times, this could actually be the correct action if solid parameters were not put in place beforehand, thus the concept of the leadership spring. But, unfortunately, I cannot say that this is always the case.

Say a crew member abuses a certain privilege, such as company vehicle use or does not properly use funds on travel and incorrectly completes the expense report. Many times, when this is brought to the attention of a leader, they act like a manager, which is why I call it "shotgun management." A manager may say, well, since this guy does not use the company car wisely, there will be no more company cars, or he might create a new policy further restricting the use of the company car for everybody.

Here's another example. The manager of operations, upon return from her trip, did not do the right thing on her expense report and, frankly, falsified it. Now an avalanche of policy revisions comes down, making it more difficult to even file an expense report, creating more man hours to review, and increasing company costs. It also enacts further restrictions, perhaps on things that can be purchased and/or reimbursed by the company!

You know I am right; sadly, I have seen this time and time again, and I am willing to bet you have as well.

We are all then considered to be liars and cheats, ineffective personnel, and problem children because two people did the wrong thing. Management pulls out a policy "shotgun" and shoots us all because we are all guilty by association!

We have discussed earlier that managers do things right, but a leader will do the right thing. You are a leader, so do the right thing.

Leaders will operate differently. They will not reach for a shotgun. Leaders are springs and operate with calibration and precision and with their principles. A leader will reach for a sniper rifle.

The leader examines the problem with appropriate detail, perhaps doing a root cause analysis, asking, "How did the problem happen in the first place?" The leader desires to shoot or fix the problem, not the people of the organization. The leader will check the machine or organization to ensure proper operating parameters. More than likely, the problem is that person who did the wrong thing. The leader addresses this individual. Perhaps termination is required, or lesser discipline and retraining are appropriate.

The leader will fix the problem, address the problem individual, and fine-tune the organization, making the situation a lesson learned. Going forward, the situation improves and, once properly addressed, has a smaller chance of reoccurring.

Flexibility is an option of the spring as it operates within the given parameters. Leaders can of course be flexible as long as they operate in a range of consistency. Sadly, most of the time, some leadership can only be perceived as consistently inconsistent!

Details and situations are different and in many cases require proper judgment to be applied. It is true that no two situations are exactly the same. Therefore, the spring and the parameters of the leader and the organization must operate in a consistent manner and be predictable so the crew can always behave and conduct themselves appropriately.

I have seen many good managers in my career who are not good leaders. While this is acceptable and there is great value in good managers, I have seldom met good leaders who were not also good managers.

Managers manage stuff—budgets, equipment, etc.—*things*, in other words, not *people*. You never manage people; they are not robots.

Great leaders know instinctively they are in the "people business." They therefore lead people and then apply those people and leadership concepts, such as those in this book, and then integrate things and stuff.

Fundamentally, the three working parts of any organization are leadership, training, and resources.

Everything begins and ends with leadership—always has, always will.

Training is paramount because even the best crew must be effectively and properly trained.

Every type and style of organization must have the necessary resources to get the job done. Whether equipment, funding, buildings, tools, vehicles, whatever the case may be, having the proper resources is paramount for any organization to succeed.

On my crew I desire the great leader who can manage "stuff" well.

I desire the great leader who can examine a crew, maximize their talents and skill sets, apply the appropriate levels and types of resources, and then apply the necessary and forward-thinking leadership concepts and principles to take the crew on a successful operation.

I bet you desire this as well. Who would not?

As a leader, the sooner you accept you are in the people business, and the sooner you realize you must lead and not manage people, the better off you will be.

Again, I desire to serve with a great leader that a crew will gladly follow and can manage the organization's "things" as well.

You can be that leader, so let's get to it.

Lead on...

"THE ROPE"

Leaders are ropes. Crew members hang on you. You provide the ability of many people to do many different things.

Why should a great leader see herself as a rope, of all things? Why do I say that people hang off of you? It could be because they actually do.

Leaders are in the people business and are therefore connected to their people in so many ways. We just discussed the concept of the spring, but regarding ropes, there are many more principles applying to leadership.

The first concept is related to rescue rope operations. When rescuers are "on rope," they are loaded with weight applied to the mainline rope. This could be the normal working relationship of the leaders and her staff. They are anchored to the leader and have leeway within the parameters of the organization to move about and all around, getting their tasks accomplished.

But there is also a secondary rope called a "belay," which is at least equal in strength to the primary rope but is not loaded with any weight applied. This creates a formidable safety net and is designed to catch any failure from being catastrophic. If the main line is compromised or fails, the belay line, or safety line, is there to prevent a fall.

So in a broader sense, leaders have two ropes attached to the crew member as they go about their business: the main line and the belay.

The concept here is that people make mistakes. Not a single one of us is perfect—never have been, never will be.

Great leaders know how to rig and design the system to allow for a crew member to grow, learn, and function well as part of a crew or own her own.

One of the greatest gifts a leader can give her crew is the ability to go out on rope, be free to exercise their skills. But if they fail, there is a safety net in place that will catch their mistake and prevent a catastrophic failure. This is done by having proper redundancies and system checks in place with other crew members and leaders. Policy and procedure come into play where, as things roll along, there are parameters in place to assure the machine or crew is operating properly.

A few years back I was at a training event with one of the organizations with which I serve, and a crew member from another part of the country complimented our team. He said to me, "You guys function like a well-loiled machine." I smiled and thanked him for his kind words on behalf of our crew as their leader, and then I did the following.

I first said a silent prayer of gratitude that I serve with such fine people. I was thankful for the opportunity to lead these crew members, which I considered as a gift.

I then looked in the mirror and did a gut check and confirmed that such kind words were received in such a manner that allowed me to stay humble and teachable.

I mentally went through the tools and concepts in my leadership toolbox and applied and learned the lessons from those kind words. I reviewed what it took in the form of investment in the crew to achieve the compliment.

Then later on, I shared those kind words with the crew and acknowledged their efforts and bragged on them for staying humble and teachable. I praised their solid efforts to lift each other up as they go about lifting up others and doing their tasks. We practice the concept that all of us must function as leaders at every level in the organization. Remember, every member of your crew is a leader, a rope. The only question is at what level do they serve? All the ropes are tied together in the organization.

The next concept of the rope is the knot that is tied to attach to anchors, carabineers, other ropes, etc.

All ropes have a tensile strength—the amount of weight the rope is designed to support. Rescue personnel function well below this tensile strength, and when a knot is tied in the rope, the rope strength is reduced by as much as one half. Ropes have to be attached someway, as we have established leaders are ropes.

Knots are relationships.

There are knots, and then there are life safety knots. Every member of a crew should be allowed to review and challenge a tied knot. We call an improperly tied knot, a "what knot." In other words, "What the heck is that? That knot does not pass muster!"

On my boat, I tie only life safety knots. With my crew, I tie only life safety knots. On a mission of any kind, we tie only life safety knots. Why? Because our lives, the task at hand, and our working relationships depend on this rope and its knot.

Knots represent relationships.

Leaders are in the people business, and they are the ropes attached to people and the organization. Crew members will anchor off of you as they go about their duties. You are, many times, the mainline and the belay.

I mentioned earlier in our time together that we don't really have jobs, we have relationships.

What is the quality of your knots, your relationships?

People quit people, and people stay with people, many times in the widest variations of conditions, both good and bad. Are your knots and relationships tied correctly? Your life, your career, your marriage, your friendship, you overall well-being are *tied* to your relationships or your knots!

If you don't recognize a knot, challenge it, declare it a "what knot": unsafe and improperly tied. Repair it and tie the knot or relationship again if you are able.

It is the leader's responsibility to repair the knot if at all possible. Part of the burden of leadership is that leaders do the right thing. I realize that sometimes it's not possible, but if you dare to lead and it is within your power, repair that relationship.

Tie that knot again. If you have done your part, then that is all you can do. Move on with grace and dignity, persevering to always learn and do better next time.

Leaders are ropes and they tie knots. What is the condition of your ropes and knots?

Lead on...

"IDEAS"

Far and away, this is one of the most powerful tools you posses in your leadership toolbox. By now surely you can see that all the tools work together for the common good of the crew and your organization.

An idea, measured against your other tools, is a powerful force.

Your ideas, are tools themselves, very creative powerful tools.

Combined with a great idea, the creative power of leadership, artistic in its very nature, can summon the greater good and the universe in general and change the course of things.

The idea alters the course of history especially when applied with the many wonderful principles of our universe.

A single grand idea can turn an organization upside down and perhaps turn failure into a roaring success.

Talent knows no rank, and anybody can change the course of things with a single great idea.

Dr. Peter Drucker said, "Rank does not confer power or give privilege. It imposes responsibility." If this is true, then every single crew member, top to bottom, if you will, shares the responsibility to create and share ideas for an organization's success.

Do you, as a leader, have the courage to listen to you crew and to implement their ideas if they are better than yours?

Great leaders do. They examine their entire toolbox and bring the tools together for the greater good. Their egos are in check.

I have heard the word *ego* defined as "edging God out of your life." I am not preaching, by any means, but I like this definition.

If you have an ego problem, your values have become "all jacked up." You are too important to yourself; perhaps you should step back, not take yourself too seriously, get back on the planet with the rest of the human race, and reboot your efforts.

Your ideas coupled with faith and proper leadership can move mountains. Entire companies, nations, teams, armies, designs, products, research—everything can be changed with a single idea.

What are your ideas?

Leaders know the immense value of ideas! They foster an environment where ideas are welcome if not required.

Ideas are foundational.

Ideas enable change for the greater good.

Ideas create, for all of us, another and better world.

Leaders cherish ideas—no matter where they come from!

Lead on…

CONCLUSION: THE BOX

Many times when I am teaching a class, I will ask the students if they consider themselves leaders. I always get mixed results. Some say yes, maybe, most certainly, perhaps, I want to be—and the list goes on.

The answer is that you are indeed a leader, even if you are just leading yourself. But this is a test question. Don't miss it.

The sooner you realize that even if you think you *aren't* in a leadership position, you must accept that you *are* indeed in a leadership position. Why?

Because you will come in contact with other people, as most of us do, and you will have the opportunity to *influence* people's lives, hopefully in a positive, uplifting manner.

If there were a one-word definition of leadership, that word would have to be *influence.*

Leadership is about your *influence* on and around others. Great leaders are aware they have enormous power over other people's lives and that they truly do have the ability to *influence* those they come in contact with.

This leadership toolbox contains tools and concepts—what some would call "things"—to get you to think. As a tangible reference point, the tools provide many vital concepts of applied leadership. But there is one remaining tool:

The box itself.

You, as the leader, are the toolbox.

The concepts we have discussed togeher in this book are all designed to be carried and used inside of you—every day.

The rubber band around your box (yourself) is designed for you to stretch your mind as you open your box (yourself) and pontificate on these tools and concepts.

My wish for you is that you have the courage to apply these concepts daily with those you have been given the awesome duty and privilege to lead.

I challenge you to lead out. I declare and ask for a special blessing for you as you lead and use the tools in this book with your crew and for the greater good of all mankind.

You, dear reader, are custom-made. You are precious and special in the eyes of someone and probably many, even if you don't know it.

We all have heroes. Are you willing to be one for somebody? To be a mentor to somebody?

That's not to say you are wimpy, not executive or CEO material, not director, commander, captain, or general officer material, not tough enough like a sergeant, drill instructor, boss or chief!

Many times true peace, prosperity, success, and the freedom to pursue happiness came from a leader who was *tough enough* yet *compassionate enough* and used the tools in this box and many others to improve the lives of others.

My wish is for you to use and apply all things that are good. Fulfill your destiny. Realize the awesome potential you have to affect the lives of others.

My wish is for you to apply the twenty-three concepts and tools—"things"—contained herein.

My wish for you is for you to lead.

Thank you, fellow leader, for spending your precious time with me.

Lead on...

About the Author

Ted Rogers is a lifelong student of leadership, whose diverse career has spanned more than thirty years of leadership experience, holding executive and senior command positions in numerous organizations in both the public and private sector. He has four degrees, including a master of science degree in administration and leadership. The author brings together the principles he has learned in his professional life in *The Leaders Toolbox: Applied Concepts of Leadership*, an easy-to-read reference book for all supervisors in any field for both the public and private sectors.

Made in the USA
Coppell, TX
20 February 2021